RUPTURE ANTHEM

PITT POETRY SERIES

NANCY KRYGOWSKI AND JEFFREY MCDANIEL, EDITORS

RUPTURE ANTHEM

HERA NAGUIB

UNIVERSITY OF PITTSBURGH PRESS

Published by the University of Pittsburgh Press, Pittsburgh, Pa., 15260

Manufactured in the United States of America
Printed on acid-free paper
10 9 8 7 6 5 4 3 2 1

ISBN 13: 978-0-8229-6840-5
ISBN 10: 0-8229-6840-1

Cover art provided by the author
Cover and book design by Melissa Dias-Mandoly

CONTENTS

III.

IV.

RUPTURE ANTHEM

November 2003

The moon, a karambit,
drags the foggy sky.

On the kitchen table,
fruit slices, like moist

claws, sit stacked
in the bowl. Mother speaks

to me, *last night,*
your father made a choice,

leave this country or go to jail.
Her words skid into

the precipice that splits between us.

It is Ramzan, moments
before the Maghrib azan filters

down the laundry lines.
The first screech flocks

in my breastbone and
my diaphragm, a slingshot,

holds on. I am sixteen.
Already I marvel at the vivid

fact of shared blood,
shot with a shock

that I imagine is
Father's. Ask me how I left

that country and I
will tell you the same way

shale cracks under slickwater
or the same way vapors, primed

for uncharted dispersals,

shed entire salt flats. In my mouth,
this secret wires and rewires itself.

Open, you ask. My mouth,
a rancid fruit, splits open.

I.

Your absence has gone through me
Like thread through a needle.
Everything I do is stitched with its color.

—W. S. MERWIN, "SEPARATION"

The Expulsion

> For there is a time in the tide of the heart, when . . . we ask, O God, where is our home?
>
> **— Derek Walcott**

That summer, the locusts coughed red dust.
We packed the house and off the sofa's gridiron,
wiped limp afternoons, matte spatter of soup
knocked by our child elbows diving first
for the TV remote, silt of arguments,
and years Father hollered to Maradona's instep kick.
Father, who shivered desert storms to a whisper
each time he hummed for us aaj mausam bara
beimann hae bara beiman hae,
aaj mausam. Father, like the sea,
an expatriate that carries on despite this country's
covert disposals. That summer, father
tucked our passports close, a prosthesis. Two
plainclothes men cocked a gun at him, trawling
our house for his residence permit.
Their fingers leeched the ventral dimness
of closets with blame. Those last nights in Jeddah,
I watched him through the parted doorway,
its narcotic eye blearing the hooded lamps,
his shoulders simmered antennal to hazard,
his forehead cleaved, like the frontier
that threshed us back to Lahore, to its grease, & gangly
boys who beggar bagged goldfish
that eyed me obliquely from plump neon waters.
Most days, as Father idled the hour content
as a windblown shack, I pendulated,
thick with rot. Superfluous, my reluctant
music of leaving, and my lies
yes, we left my birthplace, we hated the weather.
What happens when we snipe truth, its hair-narrow bridge?
What happens when we spill fictions?

Belonging, once terra firma, crumbles to smoke.
Mongrel, I huddle on rooftops, dog the city's last engine
that drones home. The red eye that blinks blinks
at the billboards' insomnia. All night,
the koel vibrates, irking the sleeping hopes of larvae.
Supine, shirtless laborers snore into the puckered moisture.
Father flicks past the news, like the news. How pathetic,
I think, how much like greed,
in these damp enervations, my private alphabet of loss.

Jeddah

Paleolake of
the gone
girlhood,
of a father's
ambition.
Sand-starved
I bedouin
through time,
yet time,
a broken caravan,
stagnates in me
& my infant
screech clamors out
anomalous as
a flood
among dunes,
frictious as
the distant
movement
of beasts
I jackal-shadow
for the carrion
of your highways'
tyranny, your
cacti prick,
Mega-stores, &
your Mejdool dates
pyramided,
like an eyeless,
dispelling god
for whom I have
smashed
my itinerant feet.

Human Capital

Tide-slurped, the shore
    rocked my father's thirst,
eyed the day he, too, will
    foray fishwards, his spine
full-mast, borderless as salt,
    the ocean beneath him
his own deep-storied calling;
    waters whistling, whistling
for weeks the big catch no
    matter the bribing coastguards,
no matter the sea-gods'
    cussing. My father thrummed
for distant coasts, tax-free
    income, the day he too
will whip up some concrete
    house on his shoreside
to vie for, a boy too green
    to read what the ocean
before him archives: assets,
    seized passports, obscene
fees the middle-men pimp from
    those lost to richer shores,
lost, in thousands, to mega
    cities they raise with ripped
palms, to filthy labor camps
    at the backwater where,
ten to twelve, they sleep, hemmed
    in by stray cats, rations,
and roaches. But a boy, my
    father hungered, as a boy
will, for he knew the sea
    is a tycoon, glib as oil,
and from eastward, it hovered
    and it murmured his name.

The Bride of the Red Sea

The hours, a desert, ran wasted.

My mother stared out at the new roads and freeways.

Gloss of urban sprawl the Americans laid out

ushered in the new. Not a being out there palpated

into sight. She fluffed tissue into roses, plucked

hair from floor tiles. Time sat fixed,

like a sacked king. From Urdu digests,

lurid contraband from Lahore,

the front cover women leered at her, some

knowledge clenched in their teeth.

This was before Father came home,

steaming flatbreads in tow. Before reruns

of *Awdat Asoid* and her bumbling Arabic.

Before the friends and the picnics by the sea.

Before the oil boom bloomed

into skyscrapers, mega-stores, and bizarre

monumental sculptures surged

everywhere. She was twenty-two, newlywed.

in the city they called the bride of the turquoise sea.

Her restlessness, prehistoric, chafed

under. She hadn't known such loneliness.

She had yet to taste loss, its precise axle.

The Bribe

Just a girl I'd gawk away

at the pool's shifting azure

until one day I toppled inside

and the horror of it choked

my sleep nights in a row. For my sweet

life then, I didn't swim, but for okra

I squatted by the pool's ledge,

my floaties billowed up on my arms,

my palms clutched at the bars. I thrashed

each time my father waded closer to pull me in,

his reaching limbs rousing the water,

and the water protean, with shadows booming

as if untrammeled by anything else,

least of all me and such assurance

the water held, such knowledge

of its murk and ploy,

like my mother who would

sit by the spitting stove fire,

her hair frizzed as if piqued by her temper

each time I told her I wouldn't swim and

she said *oh, you will,* her eyes full of

the old bribery, fingers slicing the heap

of okra, the sweet, sizzled okra

she cut open, with its pods, like gondolas

of slime and each fried aril she pushed in

like my will, the reluctant stowaway of the night.

Bildungsroman

It was not paradise until my expulsion,
my girlhood country.

Days the couch is the only promised land,
I take off, climb the campus hills

(the verbenas, like dopey supplicants,
bend to my knees) and I remember it again—

its scraping garbage cats, herbaceous
nights, like cousins, tickling my false starts

& the shuddering butterflies I pinched
in my fingers. Because I was good at fading

I slipped behind them,
made alibi the printed fauna on my frock,

taped my breasts flat, uncitizened
my femininity until I blossomed

to a blazing violence that had to speak.

Lessons from the Quran Teacher

Still on nights slammed in sweat,
as on my thirteenth summer,
what haunts: hellfire the quran
teacher warned of, the strapped
heels, the flaming braids for my white
lies, for Mondays I squandered
to Rick Dees Top 40s, death-wish
I hurled my head for in water,
& for each look the boy and I
scalloped from the backseat
of the school bus as the Jeddah heat
flexed in the rose finch's gullet,
the petunias flared their frills,
and the teacher, dim echo
in mind, yelled out—
the first glance at a man is an accident,
the second glance is haram.
But how quickly a girl
cottons to her own
concealment—evenings I'd spill
an abaya over a pale kameez
hugged at the midriff,
heady with nicotine,
and the chuka chuka
chuk warmth of needles
punching holes in the moist
cavity of a tailor shop.
How quickly a girl learns
only the inanimate will give
to passion, like the feckless dark
I would meet him in,
of empty houses shaded by
the touch-me-nots;

the discarded tables and cots
intuiting our limbs,
both Muslim,
both teenage and urging—

En Route to Mecca, My Crisis of Faith

My sisters and I row up like duckpins
in the backseat. The car belts down
the freeway, past Jeddah, past barren
mountains, and the tamarisks that sway
to the twang and beat from
the radio Mother mutes, yells *it's unholy!*
But I can't tell what's holy
from the wet glitter of appetite—
in this country, this fuel-ripe desert
that towers with drills pounding
fossils to froth for the tireless
alchemy of oil barrels and guzzling
ocean pipes. Each month here
is as the other. New skyscrapers gleam
and rival with minarets that call
Come to success!
Here I am! I bellow back.

Wheeling the Ka'aba's marbled

grounds, a gullible pilgrim, I pledge,

labbayk Allah-humma labbayk,

here I am, o Lord, here I am,

while my own tongue hymns

to the ramshackle food

stalls brimming the mosque's

farthest edge, each kebab squelched

in the humid conch of bread.

II.

Rupture Anthem

The girls and I linger in abandoned
houses, rooftop cabins, sleepy backyards.
The recreation center's locked kitchen door

we slip behind to kiss—my Arabic
broken, his English scrambled. Tipped
over us, robed in black and gold, the gild-

framed king smiles into our wedge
of darkness. I am fourteen, in love
with desert breezes, weathered shells,

dead batteries. Everything pleasurable
is haraam and we do it anyway:
sex chats with the music store's

salesman, prostrating for the one girl
I loved and lifting uniform skirts,
Abdel Kader blasting in the school bus,

the driver honking to distract the mutaween.
Each of us, at home everywhere and
nowhere, dream of the big life until

one of us who can't opens
a racing car's door and rolls onto
the road. We find her again,

her caramel arms whipped dry,
thick hair chopped, chaperoned,
detained, like the Arabian

princesses in books I smuggle past
airport security. I gorge on them, riding
to school, the shrikes tearing

through mollassesed sleep while,
around me, doused in petrodollars,
the Jeddah desertscape blooms

with bougie cars and palatial hotels.
From the labor of migrants, this veneer
                    squeaks clean—

Prologue to Womanhood

Because dirt, my father said,
wore my human face,
into the window
of the abandoned home
where the boy and I
beetled miscible, like a trick
through the teeming dark.

Because I bared my spine
for his fingers' drizzle
stirring its soft gnarls,
prying away the alarm
a woman comes
to know is her body.

Because in dining rooms,
aunties gathered to unscramble ayahs
and surveille immaculate windows
for unscarved girls,
their ringed forefingers
always heady with blame.

Because I hastened, a flash,
a mistake of speed.
And no matter how many times
I summoned foot to foot
for the untimely symmetry
of prayer, night after night,
swarming like locusts,
gregarious as Armageddon,
came the apparitions: my father,
siphoned forth in the antiseptic light,
watching the boy and I,
like a sore, expelled from the center.

How easily I believed him,
smothered for months
that dark room beneath
the arsenic trail of my
own isolate fault and bowls
of pistachio ice cream snug
between my criminal thighs.

Morning Assembly

Entire kingdom we chorused
for in the school hall, our pleats
ironed out, nail paint
scraped clean, girl-tongues taut
beneath the full-mast flag,
blading into the foreign anthem—
يَا مَوْطِنِي! O my homeland!
O aegis O emblem of creed O
scimitar burnished and
waving over steppes we
were birthed from, our sex
second-rate, propagated for
the boot bat baton
sometimes even by a mother
nodding behind, our sex
containment divinifying your land
O feudal, consider a pledge so
clamorous it avalanches anger
once igneous spitting
molten O falconer, though
each morning we hallowed
the anthem, I was bootstrapped;
in your grip, froth and
orifice, velocious cloud-
ash, biding your time—

New Jeddah, 1992

Riding along the coastal corniche,
I marveled at Joan Miro's bird-

woman blazing bronze before
the glittering sea. All beak, thighs,

and breasts. How did it get here
was a question that never startled

my mind despite the moral police
surveilling each limb, my naked hair,

or lovers caught behind windshields.
Even the trapped girls who were left

to burn in the school fire haunted
up an inquisition. *Why weren't*

they covered, the police asked back.
In sleep, I've plucked their burns,

but the charred tissue never implored
me: *how did she get here?* Even

if the residual panic clamped me down.
How did we get here? I had fallen

for the vague promises of kings, a
desert cosmopolitan, its shock

of the new. *Bustling petrodollar*
kingdom, a new age, surreal cityscape

of desert monuments, the newspapers
read. Happily, I rolled to Lafuente's

giant mosque lamps over empty
vistas, high noons ripped with fast

cars. My dumb fingers rippled
the racks on Megastar aisles as I sang,

we are the world, we are the children!

In This Country, The Future Will Never Sleep

I.

Decked in robes caramel as the whipped,
Maldivian sands, the clandestine sands

of his bacchanalian resort parties, as the
models he ships from the globe over,

the Crown Prince, the dimpled king to be,
announces on TV *Saudi Arabia's vision*

for the future. The vision is a simulation
of cities with floating ports, hectares

of theme parks, an infinite pool suspended
over the Red Sea, luxury islands, electric

flying ships and airborne taxis. And to kick
it off, footage of the first-ever Grand Prix

flashes Pharell who shreds a concert stage.
Into the wilding crowd, he shouts. Beneath

glitzy chandeliers and across buffet lamps,
the Crown Prince continues: *we will*

transform our unique strategic location
into a global hub . . . into the gateway to the world.

II.

At first, these prospects sound
too good to be true. Molten gold.

Futuristic cities. Travel overseas.
Tax-free income. Lodging and food.

Sponsored Hajj. The migrations
begin. Debt-ridden, cash strapped,

with houses sold for plane tickets,
visas, fee upon fee, the migrants

arrive from planes and seas to build
trillion-dollar cities. Rogue agents,

lone sharks, with wallets bloated,
drip with lies, *this payment proves*

you're keen—Some are warned it
won't be easy, it will be risky.

In the claws of obscure contracts,
they come without training into

the labyrinth of airports, a new
language, and roads—

III.

They come from hill-faced houses.
Fishing villages. Organic kitchen
gardens. The clean mountain air.
They come from cattle sheds.
Shut down factories. Gun-rattled
streets. Drought. From families
they leave for years on end.
Sometimes sole breadwinners,
they come from dreams as tall
as the dazzling, miles long skyscrapers
they watch on YouTube. From
regular channels. Clay houses. Bribed.
Bought. Trafficked. In millions.

IV.

Security guards. Gardners. Cooks. House help. Nannies. Taxi Drivers. Car painters. Tailors. Cleaners. Builders. Cargo ships. Shepherds. Caretakers. Farmworkers.

V.

On the northern tip of the Red Sea
lies an untraversed frontier

rippling with treacherous
terrain, rugged mountain landscapes,

untouched beaches and coral reefs.
There, the labor begins. Cramped

in eternal commutes, clouded in dust
and diesel fumes, in a digger, piling rocks

and dirt in tunnels for hours non-stop
in tunnels, he reveals: *I level the ground. I dig.*

The tasks keep changing. You won't
hear of those on cranes, who stand under

the scorching dome of desert hours, children
at times as young as eight, driving trucks.

They arrive, able-bodied, mostly men,
who excavate for such towers of babel,

then disappear on end.

VI.

There exists a city built by labor, most men, who disappear. . . .

. . . sometimes in the Arabian heat, to acres of deportation centers packed, in hundreds, with migrants. *Vectors of a virus*, the government calls them, though it means *disposable laborers.* They're rounded up from homes, arbitrarily detained, cramped in rooms littered with juice boxes, cigarette butts, and sleepless nights. There, a plastic bag swathes a corpse. A boy dangles dead from a barred window. Another burns the lice out of his hair.

VII.

Occupational injury: *His body was smashed by the weight of the heavy blocks.*
Declared Cause of Death: Unknown.

Occupational injury: She stepped on an open wire—
Declared Cause of death: Cardiac arrest.

Occupational injury: *He had no prior experience operating this type of giant machine. Maybe the blade got jammed but he did not notice that the blade was running in the upper side. He put his head inside the machine when the blade suddenly started running. At that point his head got cut by that blade and became detached from the body.*
Declared Cause of death: Uninvestigated

Occupational injury: Nosebleed. Renal failure. Dehydration. Dizziness. Vomiting. Rash.
Declared Cause of death: Natural.

VIII.

Mostly, I ached for my village's mornings,
 the tin roof that was drilled with rain,
my baby's first tooth drooling into a tomato,
 the peal of her first laughter loping
along clammy hills. I slept on a carpet
 in their children's room. I worked
for eighteen hours. Three stories. Seven
 children. No day off, no phone.
I was always hungry. Sometimes,
 when the family left, the molding
hours whittled to the question
 of escape. But my passport was taken.
What I left for: money for land
 on which I'd house my mother.
It was worth it. It could have been worse.

Brother,

Across this house, as if out of nowhere,
I hear your voice—hoarse, fibrous,

like broom bristles on wet porches
on mornings. Days you were

a toddler, I hid from you
in the bushes. Your nose tensed up

like the milk's skin under my fingertips.
Bury your phone in your pocket,

as you rush to leave,
think of the boy ambushed at the storefront,

shot through the eye, the figure wheeling past
with his phone in fist. Think of other

brothers' bodies: turgid sacks heaved
by the river's toxic belly,

blood splattered over classroom
doors, shrapnel, and swings.

Think of those who never come home or
those who saunter back through the clefts

of quieter nights haunting the margins
of our sleep; those scaling the brief transits

between the dying and the living to ask
for the scent of Eucalyptus,

tie knots, wicket stumps, and ink.
Here is some money as you step out

and here on my lips, this prayer,
though you fuss how to feel

watched is to feel small as I watch
your swift and unheeding legs

blade over the zinnias
on the path outside widening.

Repatriation Trepidation

Drenched wheatgrass over
the prison floor, the sedated
limbs of men twine, migrants, guiltless,
without trial for years, the whistleblower
behind the camera reveals. Each shriek,
a dragged hook claws at me to screech
our own could-have-beens. For twenty
winters I've curdled mute in shame
across continents, unwived entire
plains riding from airport to airport;
each psychedelic truck
that blared past Lahore's highway.
I haven't witnessed the baton
of exile but what relief,
what revolt I want to spew, like Loujain
in the film, who hurls up and drives
in protest to the Saudi border,
her gaze steadied at the penumbral
thrill spread onto the night that canopies
over the lit causeway. *I was silent for too long*,
she smiles darkly into the camera, *I thought*
I'd disappear. She peels her brocade scarf,
its swaying tip, from the dissident wind
as the two of us brace for what hazards
ignite beyond the last turnpike
and its looming choker of burning lights.

Exit Stamp

Before we left Jeddah, we swept
the house's bald marble floors, a subcontinent of walls,

oiled out in their place a new vocabulary for leaving:
freight containers, khuruj nihai,
immigration points.

Occasionally, in the next room, I'd hear Father's dry sigh.

I've orbited twenty-five cakes, but still it riles me:
Father at the doorstep, saying: *we must leave the country,*

and the two armed men who flanked him, plain clothed as trees.

I'd sprawled at my bed's foot, a parenthesis split and capsized.

If I could rumor to permanence that place, Jeddah,
I couldn't leave yet: the housing compound, the high gate

where nights a first lover tilted fist to ear,
mouthing, *call me.* The baqala, its sandwich ice creams.

Sculpture past sculpture I snoozed by on my way
to the airport now rising before me
like expelling castles.

In the new country, I'd gulp paani puri,
puke flattery, ape talk of the good tailors,
the rotten politicians (right, always, the rotten

politicians). Still I shadowboxed myself,
banging the mind's black window,
the silence hemorrhaging in me—
If you could cut yourself,

If you could cut yourself from this puzzle,
this puzzle—at passport control, my father who
shackled a smile at the officer
gavelling the final exit stamp.

If you could—
if I could erupt,
my love stroking those skies with fire—

My Father Talks to Me About Endurance

Make no mistake: this was

a steep trial and I passed it,

my hand laid over that old

life I was done with & the human

face, that cadaverous lake

I blew from my shame,

fell bare, and I picked it up

from the red ground

and offered it with hope

to new borders,

new waters.

III.

The Enigma of Arrival

I.

Singed garlic clenches the repatriated December fog.

A troop of ants shift cities,
trophy the quivering roach on their heads.

Here, there is no logic to trees tangled with fabric and electric wires.
No rhythm between the peddler and the silky Land Cruiser.

I toss fries at a murder of crows, patron opportunists of this
ancient city. I pray to their occult cawing.

Wire mesh filters the clatter of a fallen wicket,
children's screams.

Nostalgia, I am reminded, is an airborne parasite.

I lean into its arrhythmia, its tacky gossip.

II.

All day, rain hammers its exodus

bending trees to pledge for mercy.
In adjacent rooms, I shave bamboo pens, etch wooden boards.

I spell myself into absences.
As a lizard slowly sprouts its severed tail,

tissues blooming to new muscle and cartilage,
I, too, seek new ways to resurrect myself,

exile my old tongue
from my mind's stubborn colony,

its whirring nothings.

I learn a slow hermeneutic of return.

Lahore Nocturne

after Tarfia Faizullah

Here, by this tide of waste
scorched across fields,
parched grass a girl
gnaws then tosses in

a straw sack; here, by my
own body, bludgeoned
with the *stop, stop,*
stop of the commando's

thrusting gun—here, by
this hue of dawn flung
outside the fruit shack;
acknowledge loss: this

boy who twirls bracelets
of jasmine on a broken
arm, this crow peeling
a knot from a pole

in the shrine, drowned
girls in clippings
of a local newspaper, I
return to you, city where

time bloats and thins,
and time, diseased,
vomits one day after
another. Give me a way

to come back whole.
Give me a name
for the surge at the sight of
every jilted thing.

Seize me with the settling
ghost of your river,
            its spirit of relinquishment.

The Interview

—Lahore, Pakistan

I shuffle past the school's fortified metal,
guards who frisk me

with a ledger for my name,
my phone number, & why I'm here—

Default procedure,
I think, heartened by their arm's gesture,

how not one pats me down,
says: *this way, madam.* This the way

a mind deadens to what once shocked—
a hundred gunned down children,

the hourly news, each soldier combing
a passing vehicle in the street reminds us,

but my vocabulary is a failure.
Where do you think we're going?

the school's principal asks me,
his office window framing

a boy in the courtyard who hits
a ball with his bat

into the blanched spring sun. *To hell* I say,
You think so? He asks, as the two of us

watch the ball soar beyond

the ghosts of jungle gyms
and barbed wire to the roof where

a sniper guard scans the distance
for whatever scares watchers into life.

Besieged City

Always, we prime for another bombing, tight-lipped before the
footage. Always, the reporter's voice climaxes with fresh details:
shattered glass,
this row upon row of corpses.
We recoil, then thrum relief at our life's dribbling meter.
Eventually, the city, too, deceives itself,
chugs on, hung in daily smog.

Off pavements, men broom dust,
like ghosts piling in the evacuating light.

Around us, the whole strength of an empty street swarms, power
that remembers nothing,
wants nothing, spurns
each muck road that fades,
murmurous of its cry, bodies jostled
in each sputtering rickshaw;
heads in each dim bus thronged
in a planetary light.

This chatter and muteness, at once, this true
theater unveiling, as per Kristeva,
what is thrust aside in order to live, shit
that life withstands, hardly and with
difficulty, on the part of death,
like the man who rams his car into a cow, his anger
a bare-knuckled fist on her rope.
On the field, he jerks her bulk
down, hunkers over &
locks her bleating
in his arm's thick cradle. He lowers the blade.
My vision squares as the
quaking earth beneath my
breath.

My mouth, a double barrel, ticks
        at my teeth & a fist in my
        ribs, clangs in place of the heart—

Self-Portrait as Mary/Maryam

I never raised a garland for being chosen
or snapped the spine of a lamb
and fried a feast on its hot blood.
I knew where I came from
I could be slunk by the river's sleeve
at night or fed to the scarab beetles
under the piling desert sand without a spit
on my father's sky. I knew where I came from
meant I must run, desolation &
the wild conviction of infant vowels
suturing through my unsaved belly,
rumoring each of my apocryphal names—
Sayyidatuna, Siddiqah, Qānita.
It does not behoove the scriptures to tell you I think
I have wasted my time, moored
to the moon winding up my blood,
fattened with dates, the holy stream &
my gunk swamping
my body. Nothing usurps you
as suddenly as the feeling of being lost.
It was not enough to be chosen,
nobody ever tells you. It was enough
to be free—

News of Another Femicide

Here, in this glassy shop
          sneered at by rat piss and
acedia, TV flashing
          images of a woman's murder
and a man who lifts
          cuffed wrists, who stares on,
eyes rheumy as a lychee.
          He barrels the question:
how could the Christian
          refuse me, a chain
that spells Allah glimmering
          vaguely down his collar.
The aunts with me pay
          no heed. We sip bottled
Cokes, stroke rare silks
          that the shop boy waters
across our laps while
          others stop to gawk, loiter
away, habitual, indifferent,
          like any of us, who easily
disremember our past
          othering—1947, with
breaths bated on charging
          trains shredding a border
between Agra and Lahore;
          this faith in whose name
the murderer kills, bodies
          too were maimed—women,
Muslim: a grandmother who
          flicked her faith behind a bhindi,
the time for homecoming
          thin as the kirpan's tip on
her throat. Another re-
          named herself Karishma,

as in a miracle, like the
            epoch crumbling in her hair.
The epoch that furs, soft
            as amnesia, the T.V. screen
bolts of banarsi, chiffon,
            the sweat of dyers' who
fringe the shop–who lift
            from steaming cauldrons
doused clothes, like a tumble
            of hair—& the faces of dead
lieutenants on billboards
            who gaze on—those martyrs
who do not bear witness—
            with whom each day we sing

tumhe watan ki hawain salaam kehti hai,
to you, the nation's winds pay salaam—

The New Nomad

Outside my window, the long season
locks horns with another day, fetters
petals in the ice. The long season,
irrefutable, urges *no more*
room here or what the Sufi was told
centuries ago, when he set foot in the
city of saints. He was handed a glass
full to the brim, but he returned it,
with a flower afloat, yanking the sun
low enough for a starving disciple
to roast pigeons. Though little
is known of him, the Sufi was no
less a migrant, like me or like that far
country that now rattles my window-
sill. All day I'll bury its omens—
the missed note, the flowers, no longer
count the days that lift and drop their
cloaks at the sill. Dread looms,
a crown of hawks overhead. All day,
the borders I pulp slice & hollow me
until the foreign number flashes on
my phone, and I tip over to answer it,
my mouth a blasted meadow,
my mouth, this shattered glass—

Kicking Up a Mess

On a hot August night,
past the colonial boys' school,
its high brick wall, my sister, newlywed,
slumps quiet in the passenger seat. Before
the wedding she moved at nights, zombie-
like, through the kitchen, rummaging
for bad carbs. Her husband asks me
if I am a 'feminist,' his mouth crooked,
but before I, who am driving, can answer,
he goes on about his 'wise aunt who says life
is a series of peaks and troughs, you never
know what is coming next, it is best
for a person to adapt.' Euphemistically,
this means to not kick up a mess. He loves
my sister all right, my sister, the breadwinner
for whom he scours dishes after dinner; asks
'are you happy? are you happy?'
This should have been redeeming for us
upper-middle class suburban Pakistani women
told to blend just right—not too stiflingly 'traditional,'
not too controversially 'modern,' but he has spoken
for our bodies—arrived, after all,
like any other man, for those bodies
in which he has never lived. Between us,
my sister and I, his words pull up
like exhaustion itself—more ancient
than we can understand
or explain against his certainty,
which, wherever it lives, I imagine,
must be a windowless place,
though solid as a fact & boarded up
against any heave and plunge of debate.
Is this marriage? I wonder, briefly,
Is it this deflation, this lithe

twist of her neck already turned away,
this swift drop of compromise?
Crossing the road, a turtle looks up and
both of them laugh, though I want to contend
it all, the whole moment, gestational and fleeting,
which begs me to take it for what it is,
and begs me to let it go—

At the Allama Iqbal International Airport

At the Departures gate, you wave away
porters who swarm and offer
to carry your luggage. A trivial choice,
you know, even if oddly defiant.
Mostly, they are affable, middle-aged men
eager for tips in American dollars.
At the ticket counter, they while away the line
of passengers, turn to ask, unsolicited,
what it's like for you, a woman, to live abroad,
alone. They're curious, without judgment.
Though this mildly surprises you,
though you know an international
airport is as cosmopolitan
as it gets; that you could reveal here, safely,
how you love each night alley,
its curfewless hours & that room
of one's own, bounteous as a fugitive tunnel,
you don't. Instead, you say karna parta hai,
one has to, shouldering necessity
or whatever it is that your mother
and her mother always made up
for themselves. Because what perplexes more than a woman
who claims her life as her own?
To this, the porters never say much.
Maybe they, too, have daughters whom
they send off each daybreak into the dank,
panting jaws of a public bus. Maybe they, too,
admit to necessity, but never the way
it may mother invention.
But when the officer scans your I-20
at Passport Control and nods at you,
laurelling mulk ki beti, nation's daughter,
you nod back at his praise,
though your only triumph to claim

is this exit ticket you clasp in fist
as the plane lifts and
breaches a gulf beneath—

IV.

Nostalgia Is a Pathogen

I halt to prior ghosts
    that well up again as sirens
            through the tracheal alleys.

            When I tell F., he says, this is America—
what you leave for her claims you back—

            the fountain veil loping
over the ribbed Red Sea I wanted
to whisper to a shiver as a girl;
little caskets of Himalayan pine nuts
I thumbed through each sulfurous winter.

It's true I bury all the cities I call
            home & wear them like the sky's
            feigned amnesia. I throb
            tedious, as the landscape outside
where each evening, the same rangy cat
licks the fungal pool in the balding grass.

What, truly, would I give for repose: to belong?
To breathe inconspicuous as a dab
on a box Mother clamps over the still humid
dinner across the globe
            where night slinks into every
            familiar katora and spoon hollow?

Everywhere, contagion shreds
our being to a minimal question, like
What if I die? Who do you love? Come back?
My answer ferments, unspoken,
            hangs over sleep, its open bracket.

On the news, grounded airplanes
heckle me with their snouts.
Through the year, we touch no one.
The earth teeths coffins en masse.

The Work of Parting

For vigil against
the evil eye, I
toss crumbs down
the drainage ditch
scavenged nightly
by the disappearing
plumage—
these creatures,
bezubaan,
the speechless,
who, as my people say,
once fed, bloom
with prayer. Lately,
I'm emptied of prayer.
Make no mistake—
I am beholden
to the day's renewed
mercies: the steady
dollar-rupee rate,
mother's healthy blood
work in Lahore—
her texts light up
my phone as I combust
the midnight digits
in America, typing
poems. But on days
I rove language

for what clocks
my tongue through
the obscure hour—
this one truth:
I want to go back—
but nothing comes.

The Season of No Return

Instead of N.'s vanishing breath,
that spring, like merlot, ran the backed up
blood she coughed out & each

masticating enzyme in her I wanted
to dig out. The earth, dug out, grasped
my crashing knees

& my palms on her grave,
cupping petals, shed, like merlot. Driving
to the cemetery, my eyes raked

the pneumonic sky for tails
of gliding airplanes I named
the way I'd elegize each

country by my flight. That spring,
the harvest blazed, birds flopped down
from the sky and like merlot, the faces

of clerics warned this to be
an omen of our time—for women,
like me, who poured in blackouts,

into slim-stemmed glasses
their merlot grief, who poured
into grief, like a colony of fruit bats,

foraging, draped in their
foreign pelt of harm. That spring,
draped in blackouts, the hours

thawed, drunk on benzene and
sour meat. I touched no one. I
out-stared a ceiling stain till it

fleeced with rot.

Rumors of An Origin

Say I was itinerant, a long cry torn from
the rain bird's throat & married
to a warning. In Jeddah, that desert,
its fair constancy I would never breathe.

∞

I was always afraid, not of thunder,
anger, nor the dead but of my sudden
unbelonging, its looming hooves, finning
vertebral knives—

∞

Say I came from a pack of girls
who dragged a lithe boy across
the gravel, the way men in plain-
clothes drag off Jeddah's migrants—

∞

No—say I scraped myself from
the crackle under the boy's back,
the payback to his big brother,
from Jeddah's dust of stones,
from my long and white silence

∞

—say I was weaned from the season's
midriff, the stench of the ground
dank with Lahore's monsoon, from
the pull of its roots. At nights, I tore
off its long canal, dried off its course,
but pent up in my people's dream,
my wrists flamed with marigolds, footfalls,
like hard-hit drums through blackouts
from the back streets.

∞

I foamed from those sewers,
froth of the old years at my
heels no more buckled dead
like grass snakes. Wind-driven
soot, mongrel boned, I leafed
out, a circle of blades,

divergent as the homes I'm from.

Ode to American Manna

O emulsifiers, cornstarch,
O synthetic herbs
O the mind tickled by herbs the mind
that mindlessly makes its mind of a home
in you, America, the mind that must
not cleave open, that spills
miles to Lahore,
to smoldering noons,
college dust & canteen fumes
decked in my hair and the funk
of the hot staircase iron haranguing
my back. O arable racks, what have you
heard of the humid scramble
of aisles thronged so close, even the quickest
rumor doesn't escape? Of shopkeepers
squatting in the shade, of the fatigue
of a homecoming that never comes?
Self-service checkout, I raise to you my
scan-and-go hungers, as you flash,
a bleating Cyclops I spray
with leafy wet, like sweat misted
on my spine entire heatwaves ago
as I slumped before my laptop display &
its once pallid island of poems,
adrift and burning.

The Years We Carry

At any rate, for us it was over—our everyday lives,
what began like an era, the first uncertain

visit to Jeddah in 1979 by a young
man named Naguib, the new language

crisp at his tonsils. Fresh asphalt of a new city
plopped out, slippery as petro-fluid.

In the mornings, the reluctant flatulence
of the school bus, our friends, mollusked

hiss of the Red Sea ramming my ear,
hot tea cakes in tow, the anomalous wind

banging the breastbone. Behind the trash can,
Louai swung me by my pigtails

in long circles. *Era, era,* he sang my name.
Marium, Abdel-Rahim. The one creased

photo of his baby son we tore in half.
Our house a sepulcher; my face, when last

towards it, wet and fossilized. The airport
that emerged, a canine & the year turning

a page we couldn't read yet, the year leaching
from its past like a father from his.

Quietly he whispered *glory to god,*
only God is glorious when I asked him,

are we poor? The sloshing pitchers of milk
I wolfed down, stolen tangerines bulging

in my pocket, happily as a goiter. As if all
of our lives in Jeddah were a lie and we had

been found out. The lace curtains I unclasped
like gauze. That one night rising, a gulp of ocean

we were flung at & a dream of my face
barreled into a bullet I homed in on Father.

In the Name of Yellow Leaves That Is My Country

زرد پتوں کا بن جو مرا دیس ہے درد کی
انجمن جو مرا دیس ہے

—فیض احمد فیض | **Faiz Ahmad Faiz**

If I could see, simply, where to get to
                    in Lahore where I stood,
blunt as a rickshaw flap.
Neither seen nor hidden—
If I had tossed
into its river's murky sleeve,
its litter floating—
If I could say one true thing to it,
like *fuck this place*

If I had said let me break free

If I could walk its river's cusp,
like the pilgrims who haunt its sludge,
who fling from gaunt arms
chunks of meat for crows

If I held out a lump and waited for one to clutch back,
          my stillness loosened—
my benevolence like grease
If the river wasn't hurt,
its toxic belly with bloated minnows,
          pharmaceuticals, and lovers routinely scavenged,
sometimes dumped

If I hadn't turned to leave
that river, that city, the wet mud
at my feet trapping rainbows,
bubbling, hissing, *you will carry this burden*:
scabbed walls, fissures,

city that daily orphans its own
miasma, flaccid mynah;
fraying the banner's slogan
the evergreen minister's grin;
or makeshift earth ovens,
with livestock and farmers razed off
          for Urban Transport and Housing schemes

If I could spin away & still sing
under each bridge's black lung
of the woman who sweeps
the pavement with one foot short
of toes sliced clean from a factory machine;
of laborers who flank the back streets,
          with backs kissed
                    to the scrape and dirt of earth,
with snores humming in the sewer
and ribs that froth
with echoes of hard-hit drums
sent from a flaring of wedding tents;
of the vagrant children who huddle
              like matchsticks in sewers,
with fists pumping needles, their bloodstream
like the raceway belted overhead;
          of the lurker in alleys who moves
panther slow, his heart a war-beat,
an artillery rattling
of those clerks who slouch
                    before strident, ringing phones,
whose imagined, impossible lives float nameless
through writhing phone cables;
          of the salon worker who softly thrums
      to Bollywood tunes, who breathes
into my supine nostril

something of fuchsia lips
                    and riflescope eyes she'll wear one day
for billboards of ghost theaters;

of the dancer who flees in time to the airport,
by the invisible rope of a blackout,
against the thought
of her own hacked body,
heedless of the hash the cleric-pimp
slips into her suitcase—
& of the activist who peacefully knocks
          municipal doors that mete out her protest
                    for clean air and water
                    in body bags or a hit-and-run;
of the drivers who daily sling in car seats
outside the boys' school to steal a last drag
of smoke before home time, before the last
chickpea dunks
into their moist newspaper cone, before their slobbering
little masters herd inside
heaving stink & orders—

of each empty hour
in which Mother spores ears
to her discontent,
its fungal wool
          & of my father, whose swilled dreams
no longer scramble before him, like TV static—

If I could speak, simply,
                              outside assonance,

If I could speak plain as tarmac
          to that shady, vigorous, fortressed city

that spills tedium like ash
and so much shit

                                        would it condescend to me,
a stone splitting my absence, its far seas?

NOTES

"The Expulsion" references lines from "Aaj Mausaum Bada Beimaan Hai," a Hindi song by the renowned singer, the late Muhammad Rafi. The poem also includes a phrase from *Notebook of a Return to the Native Land* by Aimé Césaire and from "The Muse of History at Rampanalgas" in *Sea Grapes* by Derek Walcott.

"Prologue to Womanhood" includes a phrase from "Elms" by Sylvia Plath.

"New Jeddah, 1992" references lines from the song "We Are the World" by USA for Africa.

"In This Country, the Future Will Never Sleep" catalogs the rampant migrant exploitation and abuse that has occurred under the execution of projects lined up as part of Saudi Arabia's Vision 2030 (see next note for description). Exploitation and abuse of migrant workers is though a pressing human rights issue that dates beyond Saudi Arabia's Vision 2030 programs and owes itself to the decades-old kafala system. The kafala system is a severely restrictive migrant sponsorship system that ties migrants' legal status to their employer, lending disproportionate power to the employer. Practiced in variations in the countries along the Persian Gulf, including Saudi Arabia, the kafala system has historically created conditions of extreme vulnerability to abuse, including wage theft, perilous working conditions, exorbitant employment fees, debt bondage, forced labor, confiscated passports, etc. Despite such exploitative conditions, migrant workers in Saudi Arabia represent 42% of the country's population, according to a report published in 2024 by Human Rights Watch, who have been actively documenting migrant labor abuses for over two decades. According to the Council for Foreign Relations "workers accept jobs in kafala host countries often because they offer higher pay than jobs in their home countries. Many workers then send remittances home, which the World Bank notes can help alleviate poverty in low- and middle-income countries."

Part I quotes Crown Prince Mohammad bin Salman, also known as MBS, the de facto ruler of Saudi Arabia—at the time Deputy Crown Prince and Defense Minister—from "Saudi Arabia's Vision 2030," a speech delivered on 25 January 2016. The speech announces Saudi Arabia's grand $2 trillion top-down mega-program for economic and social overhaul with the aim to reduce the country's economic dependency on oil. While reforms on women's welfare have been implemented through measures such as lifting travel restrictions on women and boosting participating in the workforce, the program has been criticized for its ignorance for the protection of political and basic human rights.

- Part V quotes from an interview with an anonymous migrant construction worker employed to build "The Line," a proposed 170 km (160-mile) linear city, a project of NEOM, a futuristic and ecological megacity led by the Saudi government costing an estimated $500 billion and the embodiment of Vision 2030. In the interview, which was published, along with a series of migrant worker testimonies in a report titled ""Die First, and I'll Pay You Later": Saudi Arabia's Giga-Project Built on Widespread Labor Abuses," and published by Human Rights Watch in June 16, 2022, the worker reveals being charged $1000 illegal recruitment fees. Of Neom, Jeed Basyouni, Middle East director of the human rights organization Reprieve, told DW that "the glossy brochures don't show that this is a city being built on forcible evictions, state violence and death sentences." For her, NEOM epitomizes the "gulf between Mohammed bin Salman's professed 'vision' of Saudi Arabia and the repressive reality of his rule."

- Part VI includes a line from *Temporary People* by Deepak Unnikrishnan.

- Part VII references an investigative report titled "Saudi Arabia: Migrant Workers Electrocuted, Decapitated, and Falling to Death at Workplaces" and published by Human Rights Watch on May 14, 2025. The report sheds light on "scores of migrant workers [who] have died in gruesome yet unavoidable work-place related accidents." The report also investigates how "many migrant deaths in Saudi Arabia are erroneously classified as "natural" and are neither investigated nor compensated. The process for compensation for work-related accidents is long and burdensome." The poem quotes an oral account by the widow of a 36-year-old Bangladeshi migrant worker who worked in Saudi Arabia for over eight years and the widow of a 43-year-old Bangladeshi man who cut concrete blocks in Saudi Arabia for two years.

"Repatriation Trepidation" includes a reference to Loujain al-Hathloul, a Saudi women's human rights activist and political prisoner who was arrested in May 2018 as well as detained and tortured on several occasions for defying the ban on women driving in Saudi Arabia. The driving ban was lifted in June 2018 as part of the reforms included in Saudi Arabia's Vision 2030.

"The Enigma of Arrival" borrows its title from Giorgio de Chirico's painting by the same name. Additionally, the poem repurposes two lines from "Chinatown Diptych" by Jenny Xie.

"Lahore Nocturne" is after "The Interviewer Acknowledges Desire" by Tarfia Faizullah.

"Besieged City" quotes from Julia Kristeva's *Powers of Horror: An Essay on Abjection* (1980).

"News of Another Femicide" references the act of masking, a common tactic survival practiced by Hindus, Sikhs, and Muslims where markers of one's religious identity were concealed to avoid attacks by violent mobs during the 1947 partition. The poem also quotes from "Aye Rah-e-Haq ke Shaheedo," an Urdu patriotic song originally sung by Naseem Begum for Pakistani soldiers who died during the 1965 Indo-Pak war. The song has been reproduced notably by Coke Studio Pakistan Season 9 for August Independence Day celebrations in 2016. While the cover garnered a widely patriotic response, critics snubbed it as standard military establishment propaganda.

ACKNOWLEDGMENTS

Versions of these poems have appeared in the following publications, sometimes under different titles:

The Academy of American Poets: "The Bribe"; *Academy of American Poets* Poem-a-Day*:* "Prologue to Womanhood"; *AGNI*: "Morning Assembly," "Rupture Anthem"; *The Believer*: "Bildungsroman"; *Beloit Poetry Journal*: "The New Nomad"; *The Boiler Journal*: "Rumors of an Origin"; *The Cincinnati Review*: "En Route to Mecca, My Crisis of Faith"; *The Common*: "Repatriation Trepidation," "Nostalgia Is a Pathogen"; *Gulf Coast*: "Lessons from the Quran Teacher"; *Hermeneutic Chaos*: "Brother"; *Iowa Review*: "Ode to American Manna"; *Michigan Quarterly Review Mixtape Series:* "Jeddah"; *The Missing Slate*: "In the Name of Yellowing Leaves That is My Country"; *New England Review*: "Kicking Up a Mess," "News of Another Femicide"; *Poetry International:* "The Bride of the Red Sea," "The Season of No Return"; *Poetry Northwest*: "Exit Stamp"; *Prairie Schooner*: "The Interview"; *Quarterly West*: "The Expulsion"; *Southeast Review*: "Self-Portrait of Maryam/Mary"; *Wasafiri*: "At the Allama Iqbal Airport"; *World Literature Today*: "Lahore Nocturne."

Thanks to all my teachers in Jeddah, Mississauga, Lahore, you believed before I believed. And in New York (at Sarah Lawrence College) and Tallahassee (at Florida State University): Jeffrey McDaniel, for your words of belief, the life-changing call, and your continual support at critical stages. Thank you to Marie Howe, Tina Chang, Mark Wunderlich, Martha Rhodes, James Kimbrell, David Kirby, Robert Stilling, Elias Dominguez Barajas, Celia Caputi, Barbara Hamby, and the late Ned Stuckey French.

To my students—near and far, current and former—thank you for inspiring me to become a better reader and teacher of literature

For the generous gift of financial support, time, and community, special thanks to Art Omi—to Emma Ramadan, Ruth Adams, Jaime Lyn Kara, and Jeremy Adams for ensuring a memorable residency and to my great cohort (Pete, Jenny, Laura, Rima, Mayte, Res, Rahel, Nicolas, Ayesha, Theresia, and Gilda). Thanks to the Sundress Academy of the Arts, especially to Erin Elizabeth Smith and to Idra Novey for your selection for the VIDA Residency Fellowship that made my stay at the Firefly Farms possible. Thanks, as well, to the Barbara Deming Memorial Fund, Boston Writers Room, GASHER Press for granting me the space and resources to write. Many thanks to the Fulbright program for a graduate scholarship that began this whole journey.

Thanks to Sally Wen Mao who chose "The Expulsion" for the 2022 *Quarterly West* Poetry Prize. Thank you to the readers and editors who selected poems to publish from *Rupture Anthem*. Thank you, especially, to Jennifer Chang and Sasha Pimental for your strong words of praise and belief.

Eternal gratitude to the wonderful people at the University of Pittsburgh Press: Jeffrey McDaniel (again), Nancy Krygowski, Alex Wolfe, Lesley Rains, Caleb Gill, Deborah Hudson, and Melissa Dias-Mandoly. I am blessed to have found a home for my book with you. Thank you to Rosebud-Ben Oni and to Raina J. Leóne for your perceptive feedback on early versions of *Rupture Anthem*.

For your friendship, care, inspiration, feedback, and community throughout the years when this book was in the making: Natasha Jozi, Amina Rizwan, Aqsa Ijaz, Haider Shahbaz, Mahreen Sohail, Miriam Nash, Laura Post, Carla Carlson, Gbenga Adesina, Esther Ifesinachi Okonkwo, Li Zhuang, Chiyon Yu, Maisha Hossain, Noorulain Noor, Sana Muzammil, and Sameen Abubakr.

And special gratitude to my family, especially my parents, Naguib and Shazia, for everything, for modelling ambition, unwavering faith, and resilience. For kindling my love of art and literature and for filling my life with books. I cannot thank you enough. To Amber, Nida, and Rafae, I couldn't have asked for better siblings; you have always celebrated me and my dreams and I am forever indebted. Our little Mikail, you are the joy of our lives and who would have imagined the healing you brought to our lives? To Nano, my late grandmother, Ghazala, from whom I inherited this dream, thank you.

And finally, to Feroz, I could not have done without your steady love and direction. I am lucky to be yours.